Through Love & Spirit, we embrace…

THE POETRY OF LIFE

L. D. ZINGG

ISBN-13: 978-1976074561

ISBN-10: 1976074568

First Edition: 2018.01

Published by L. D. Zingg, LLC

Edited by Jennifer Zingg

Cover design by John Ingle

LDZingg@gmail.com

FaceBook: LD Zingg

Available at Amazon.com

Dedication

To my wife, Lois Ann, my daughters, Cydney & Jennifer, and to my son Mark, who was called to his heavenly home while in the prime of his life. And to all who have ever lost a loved one and struggle to make sense of the world around them.

Acknowledgments

Thanks to my family and friends for their encouragement and critiques. A special thanks to my daughter, Jennifer, and to John Ingle, without whose assistance, the publication of these writings not have been possible.

Other books by this author

DESTINY OF A COP

LIARS ALL

THE LIGHT OF TRUTH

WHERE IT ALL BEGAN

Children's books

BARNYARD FRIENDS

A ROBIN INVITED ME TO DINNER

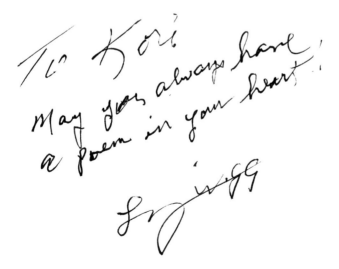

Contents

A BETTER YOU.. 1

A GRAIN OF SAND 5

A LIFETIME AWAITED 7

A REFLECTION ON LIFE 9

A SEARCH FOR BEAUTY.. 11

BACK IN TIME.. 15

FRIGHTFUL DREAMS 19

HAVE YOU EVER WISHED FOR SOMETHING? 23

I WAS HERE FOR A WHILE 25

I WONDER WHERE THE ANGELS GO............................ 27

IF I WERE YOU 31

I'LL TAKE YOUR HAND 33

IT WAS ONLY A RENTAL ANYWAY 37

I'VE GONE ON AHEAD.. 41

JUST ANOTHER FISH STORY 45

LADY LUCK.. 51

LILLY.. 53

LOST... 57

MY FATE: A CRIMINAL'S TALE & A COP'S TALE............. 59

MY SISTER ANNIE AND ME.. 63

MY SPIRIT SHALL REMAIN 67

ONE MORE FURROW TO PLOW 71

ROW ON ROW 73

SOMETIMES THE HUNTER 77

STREAMS OF LIFE 81

THE FIFTH AMENDMENT 83

THE HEAVY HAND OF FATE 85

THE OLD MAN 89

THE PERFECT MAN 93

THE SETTING SUN 97

THE STRANGER AT MY DOOR 101

THE SUN CAME UP TODAY 103

TIME 105

TOMORROW 109

TRIBUTE TO DENVER HIGH 115

WE LOST ANOTHER GOOD MAN TODAY 119

WHAT DOES A POLYGRAPH EXAMINER DO 121

WHEN I COME AROUND AGAIN 123

WHEN IS IT GOING TO BE MY TURN 127

WHO AM I? 133

These words came to me after a restless night. My mind wouldn't stop mulling over the day's events. I tossed and turned half the night and bemoaned the fact that I couldn't sleep. Early the next morning, I quit feeling sorry for myself and thanked God that I had a bed to sleep in and a roof over my head.

A BETTER YOU

Last night as I lay waiting for a sleep that wouldn't come,
My mind raced through the day's events like pounding on a drum.
I thought about the things I did and things I should have done.
Some were things I had to do and some were just for fun.

When suddenly a figure glided softly through the door.
I strained my eyes and swallowed hard and strained my eyes some more.
The moonlight through the window pane cast such an eerie glow.
I thought I must be seeing things that weren't mine to know.

My heart was beating very fast within my trembling chest.
I wanted to jump up and run, but lying still was best.
I saw the figure watching, though I pretended not to see.
I thought if I ignored him, he would surely let me be.

His eyes were burning into me like paper to a flame.
I tried my best to turn my head and think of what to blame.
Was I truly fast asleep, or was I really still awake?
Was all that I was seeing here just nothing but a fake?

Although I tried to turn away, I could not move a hair.
I closed my eyes and opened them, but the figure was still there.
He drifted closer to my bed and I could clearly see,
The stranger that I feared would harm looked similar to me.

What is this thing, I asked myself that came here in the night?
It made me shrink and made me think and gave me such a fright.
My courage took a better turn and I looked closer still.
Yes, that is me, I told myself, while using all my will.

Am I asleep? Have I gone mad? I cannot meet myself.
Yet, there we were, face to face–unless he is an elf.
An elf can take on many forms and maybe one is me.
An animal–a human–and some become a tree.

So this excuse I gave myself, but then it did not last.
For this was not an elf I see, but someone from my past.
My ego stood before me in the darkness of the night.
Running through my darker days and showing me the light.

I came to tell you who you were and who you came to be.
So listen to me close my son and you will plainly see.
The things you did and didn't do are finally catching up.
You drank from life so recklessly until you've drained your cup.

It now is time to leave the past and think what best to do,
Continue on your errant path or become a better you.
So do not dwell on what you were, but what your future holds.
And live each day to do some good as your path through life unfolds.

I looked anew at the figure standing there beside my bed.
I breathed a bit and moved a bit and straightened out my head.
For I had frozen in my place, afraid to move a hair.
And you would too, I do believe, if you had seen his stare.

A soft and lovely fragrance that I recognized to be,
Of lilies fair, sweet William too, and violets came to me.
For suddenly I understood the meaning of this night.
I faced myself to do some good and not to cause a fright.

So if you find a figure standing there beside your bed,
And it's dark and kind of gloomy and you're afraid to move your head,
Be not afraid to look around and ask some questions too.
For the person you are looking at…is just a better you.

There were times when I felt as if I had no will of my own. Like a grain of sand being pushed and pulled by the tide of destiny. Unknowing and unrefined at first, but through trial and error, I was molded into the life I was destined to lead, the job I was destined to do, and the person I was destined to become.

A GRAIN OF SAND

A grain of sand on an endless beach
At the mercy of the tide
No obstacles to face or breach
Just going along for the ride

Unfettered freedom was not to be
It was swallowed up by fate
Taken by the briny sea
No force to man the gate

Bound and blinded evermore
Without a ray of light
A darkened place so far from shore
The dull now polished bright

Formed and shaped by years of toil
Within a confined space
The clam of life released its spoil
A pearl now in its place

I don't know what prompted me to write this poem. Maybe it's because so many people are getting a divorce. Maybe it's because breakups seem to come as a complete surprise to one of the partners. Then, again, maybe it's because love is far more complicated than I am able to comprehend.

A LIFETIME AWAITED

A lifetime awaited.
A sigh of resign.
A love that abated.
No stars that align.

What is it that tells
When a love goes away,
And all loving cells
Have gone to decay?

Is there ever a sign
That would tell when it's gone?
Or must I resign
That I loved her too long?

We often spend too much time on the superficial aspects of life, and not enough time on things that are more meaningful, such as family and friends. The trouble is, we seldom realize our mistake until it is too late.

A REFLECTION ON LIFE

Don't run away and hang your head
as if to hide your face,

For somewhere in this scheme of things
we all must find our place.

All things happen as they should
as they were meant to be,

Providing all the space to grow
with room for you and me.

So cherish each and every day
as though it were your last.

Be not afraid to take a chance
and to your dreams hold fast.

Do not regret the yesterdays,
but savor them like wine.

And do not waste your life away
as I have wasted mine.

It seems we are always searching for something that is missing in our lives. Sometimes consciously, but more often than not, subconsciously. In this poem, I used the word beauty. But maybe it's love, happiness, security, prestige, or any number of things.

We don't like our job. But maybe it's our assignment, so we concentrate on getting a new assignment. But after a while, that doesn't work out, so we change jobs. No, that doesn't do it either. We need to move away and start over. So we move, thinking a new location will solve our problems. That may be true for a time. But then, the same old ache sets in. The only thing that changed is our location. The problems remain. So we buy a new car, new clothes, a new toy. But that doesn't do it.

Maybe it's our partner. We need to find someone who will make us happy. So we change partners. But after a while, we realize we've made the wrong choice, so we do it all over again…and again…and yet again. In the end, we may not be completely satisfied with choice of location, partner, job, etc., but we grow tired and settle for what we have.

Now, maybe—just maybe—our search for something more satisfying was closer than we thought. Maybe it was not to be found in some-where, or some-thing, or some-one, but within ourselves. Maybe, we were looking too hard for something that was right before our eyes. We couldn't see the forest for the trees, so to speak. These were my thoughts when I wrote the following:

A SEARCH FOR BEAUTY

I searched for beauty far and wide,
Across the desert and the raging sea.
Across the mountains and the Great Divide,
For I knew that beauty was waiting for me.

I traveled by rail by car and boat.
I flew and thumbed and walked and ran,
From cities large to ones remote.
I searched in vain through the Isle of Man

The days were long and the nights were hard.
I slogged through cold and heat and rain.
My physical health was of no regard.
I'd find my love and ease my pain.

What takes a man on such a quest,
To places he has never known?
When close at hand is always best,
If seeds are tended that were sown.

What makes him reach across the fence,
To pluck a flower growing there?
When all around is beauty dense.
Is it the excitement of the dare?

I didn't find that which I sought.
At least not where I thought it'd be.
I found my search was all for naught.
It wasn't there, at least for me.

So I returned to my own back yard.
The effort made was all in vain.
Failure is always very hard.
It left my heart with sorrow and pain.

The search that I had carried out,
Had made me think about my goal.
The prize is not in a foreign land,
Where one must pay a heavy toll.

I looked around and within arm's reach
Stood beauty right before my eyes.
Like a tree that bore the perfect peach,
My folly, I did realize.

The beauty I knew when I went away,
Somehow became that which I sought.
Why couldn't I see it on that day?
Or was it always just a thought?

So if you think you need to find
A beauty that will make you bolder,
Just look around in your own back yard,
For it's in the eye of the beholder.

Sometimes, as the sun slowly sinks beyond the horizon, daylight begins to fade, and a plethora of colors are painted across the sky, my heart yearns to be a kid again. To run barefoot through the fields of the family farm, my dog at my side. What a magical time that was.

My mother was from Holland. She kept the family tradition, including the children, of having a cup of hot tea first thing in the morning, with a spoon of sugar and cream so rich it floated on top. Then it was out the door to do chores.

Occasionally, a cow would kick our bucket over, spilling milk into the gutter. I loved the smell of everything in the barn. It was comforting. Something familiar and reassuring each time I entered the building. It was my security blanket. I was pretty isolated, living in the country, so I couldn't imagine any other life than that of a farmer.

Evenings were always a special time on the farm. Field work was done for the day. The livestock was fed. Milking was done, and we all sat down for supper. A farmer's supper, with fried chicken, mashed potatoes and gravy, sweetcorn, green beans, homemade bread with freshly churned butter, and apple pie.

After supper, when the weather permitted, the entire family would gather on the porch that wrapped around one entire end of the house and sip our coffee. The only sound would be the twill of a meadowlark, or the unmistakable call of a pheasant.

Sometimes, my dad would tell stories of life on the prairie when he was a boy. He would keep us spellbound with his graphic details of those early days. What a wonderful, peaceful, and secure feeling that was. The older I get, the more my mind drifts back to those unforgettable and magical days.

BACK IN TIME

I often wish that I could go
Back to the place I used to know,
Back to the farm where I was born
And awaken to a country morn.

Each day much like the day before.
A cup of tea then out the door.
A lot of chores and work to do.
There's feed and clean and milking too.

In the barn we had a radio
On country stations we came to know.
We sung along to our favorite tune,
But the good songs ended much too soon.

The barn would yield such familiar smells
With manure and straw that filled the wells,
The hay and grain for cattle feed,
Mixed in with milk which we spilled, indeed.

Back to a life much simpler then,
When field work was done by men
Who loved the work they did each day
And weren't in it for the pay.

Where spring presents a newborn day,
And summers' smell of new-mown hay.
A barefoot kid who roamed the fields,
And marveled at the bounteous yields.

Where fields of corn stood row on row
Pretending that they didn't know
That in the fall they'd fill a need,
For they would end up cattle feed.

The place that I would never leave
At least back then, I did believe,
Would always be the very same
Regardless of who I became.

Then, time stood still, or so I thought,
But childhood dreams were all for naught.
Though visions in my head weren't grand.
I'd stay right there and work the land.

But it didn't turn out quite that way.
I left the farm and went away
To a city that I didn't know,
And adapting to the changes, slow.

But now I've ended my career,
And who I am is much-more clear.
For I'm the sum of all I've known,
Of farm and city, of dust and stone.

For each of us can no longer be
Only what we were, you see.
We take in all that we have known,
And harvest all the seeds we've sown.

And like the crops that fill a need,
So too, are we a single seed,
That God has grown in his garden bed,
But let us choose the life we led.

But just as life for crops do end,
We cannot, like the corn, pretend.
We must prepare without a fuss
For God to come and harvest us.

Nightmares are a strange thing. Sometimes, it is difficult to separate fantasy from reality. This poem is the result of a restless night and a frightening incident. Having been a cop for many years only served to heighten my sense of awareness and, therefore, my concern.

FRIGHTFUL DREAMS

I sometimes have such frightful dreams
That seem so very real
I try to yell for help it seems
But produce a muted squeal

Monsters, snakes and ghostly things
Creep in my dreams at night
They make up what my nightmare brings
All there to cause me fright

But last night was the real thing
That ne'er a dream could match
Or the scariest nightmare ever bring
Or a terror plot could hatch

I awoke to someone in my room
In the middle of the night
The house was quiet as a tomb
Not a soul to know my plight

No words were said, but I could feel
Something pressed against my back
I have known the strength of cold hard steal
And a bullet leave its track

He hadn't uttered a single word
Since waking me this way
I wondered why I hadn't heard
Him telling me to pay

The object poking in my back
Was real as real can be
Am I to die here in my sack?
Is a bullet meant for me?

I tried to think of what to do
To counter the situation
My muscles all had turned to goo
In tune with my resignation

But any person worth his salt
Will put up one last fight
My willingness I could not fault
I'd blind him with my light

So I grabbed the flashlight on the stand
That I always kept quite near
And I swung it hard with my right hand
My strength compelled by fear

My pride now suffered quite a blow
Once I turned on the light
The weapon that had scared me so
Was finally in plain sight

The thing that shook me to my soul
That I feared would shoot me dead
Was nothing but the remote control
That my wife left in the bed

I wrote this for our youngest daughter whose attributes far exceed mine. She is the most unselfish person I have ever known, and always looks for ways to help others without consideration for herself.

Although she is a school teacher with a modest salary, she is always the first to contribute to the welfare of others.

These words are not only written from the perspective of her parents, but from the many relatives and strangers she has helped along the way. How fortunate we are to have her in our life.

HAVE YOU EVER WISHED FOR SOMETHING?

Have you ever wished for something
On a dark and moonless night,
That would give you lots of courage,
And would take away your fright?

Have you ever wished a heavenly star
Would never lose its light,
And even through your darkest hours
Would always shine as bright?

Have you ever wished the special dreams
That you have longed to hold,
Would come true as desired
And be more valuable than gold?

If all the wishes ever made
Were bundled into one
And they were destined to come true
Before my life was done

Then all my many wishes
Really did come true
For everything I wished for
Is all wrapped up in you.

I wrote this poem on a spur-of-the-moment following the death of a friend. I had no idea he was that sick. It was a shock to hear about his sudden passing. He confided in me some regrets he had, but he tried to make up for them in his daily life.

I WAS HERE FOR A WHILE

I was here for a while, but I was called away.
It wasn't my choice, but that's OK.
My body remains, but my soul is gone.
It's now in transit to the Great Beyond.

So do not grieve and do not weep,
For the life I had wasn't mine to keep.
It was only a loan for a finite time
Until I could trade for a life sublime

So judge me not for mistakes I've made.
With constant thoughts of regret, I've paid
And happiness gained was returned each day.
For it isn't ours until we give it away

Now I am in that special place where we all long to go.
Where there are no more tears, and there is no more woe.
So have no fear when it's your time too,
For I'll be there...waiting just for you.

This one came to me in 1996 after my first heart surgery and I saw how well my wife took care of me after I got home. She has always been tender hearted and helpful to others as well. I believe there is a reason for everything. This poem is the only reasonable explanation for her disposition.

I WONDER WHERE THE ANGELS GO

I wonder where the Angels go
When day has turned to night.
I wonder where their resting place
Can be when things are right.

I wonder where the Angels go
When their day's work is through.
When they are tired and weary
From protecting me and you.

I wonder where the Angels go
To soothe their aching souls.
From seeing people shun the Lord
Just to reach their lofty goals.

I wonder where the Angels go
To energize their powers,
To restore faith within themselves
In order to restore ours.

I think I know where the Angels go
To satisfy their needs,
To feel their efforts worthy,
To prepare for future deeds.

I'm sure I know where the Angels go
For I am in there too.
And even with the Angel host,
There is even room for you.

I'll tell you where the Angels go,
And it's not because I'm smart.
I know because I saw them there.
For they live in my wife's heart.

There are angelic qualities in all of us. It sometimes takes a crisis to display them.

I worked with a very intelligent man who would often correct people when they started out with "If I were you, I would do..." or, "If I were you, I would say..."

Those people always sounded so sure of themselves. So convinced that they were right. But he would tell them: "If you were me, then you would be me and you would, therefore, say and do what I would say and do." So I put it to verse.

IF I WERE YOU

I've often wondered how it'd be
If I were you, and you were me.
If I could live inside your skin
And know what's going on within.

If I could see things through your eyes,
I wonder, would I be as wise?
Would I be right and never wrong?
And always act like I belong?

Or would there be some lesser times
When things go wrong and nothing rhymes?
Would I be right, but sometimes wrong?
Sometimes weak, and sometimes strong?

The answer is as plain can be
When viewed in its reality.
We'd each be as we are, you see,
If I were you, and you were me.

This one is for all who have ever been in love,
and for all who ever hope to be.

I'LL TAKE YOUR HAND

There was a time before we met
When love was only dreamed
The promise of a better life
Was never what it seemed

The emptiness I've known so long
The depression and despair
All fade away within my mind
Whenever you are near

You make me feel so much alive
So important in many ways
Your thoughts and deeds show me you care
Your smile lights up my days

I love you and I need you so
You mean the world to me
You are my love for all my life
Unto eternity

When you tell me that you love me
My heart still skips a beat
Your love is something special
So wonderful and sweet

With passing time, it stronger grows
This love I've held so long for you
I'll show through life how much I care
In all I say. In all I do.

And when you take that final step
To another world that waits for you
Fear not, for when it's time to go
I'll take your hand and guide you through

To love someone when they are young, vibrant, and beautiful is easy. But when age and illness has ravaged their body and they no longer resemble, in manner and looks, the person they once were, that is the real test of love.

I'm not sure anyone is really ready for that final day. There are always so many things left undone. This compilation of words is a reminder that we are all transients, occupying a temporary residence we call life, until such time as we go to our permanent home.

IT WAS ONLY A RENTAL ANYWAY

An Angel came today. She didn't even knock. She just waltzed right in, even though I hadn't really invited her and I wasn't prepared for such a visit. It didn't matter. She came in anyway.

My house wasn't in order. Things were strewn about. Projects were half-done, and some weren't even started. Oh sure, I was going to get to them one of these days, but... Funny, I had plenty of reasons at the time, but I can't think of a single one now. It didn't matter. It was too late now anyway.

All I can say is that I wasn't ready for such a distinguished guest. I wonder if anyone ever really is. Some say they've been ready since birth. Maybe so. I can't speak for them. I can only say there were so many things that I had put off. I hadn't even swept. It didn't matter. Her feet never touched the floor anyway.

I was so humbled by her presence, I forgot my manners. I never even offered her a chair. I was speechless. I couldn't talk. I couldn't move. I couldn't think. My mind was racing, trying to come up with an excuse for being so unprepared.

I had put things off because I wanted to make sure that I got everything right. That's it. That's the reason I was ill prepared. If I had another day... It didn't matter. She stayed anyway.

I told her that I needed to say my goodbyes. That it was rude to leave without notice. She smiled and slowly shook her head. But there are so many things I have left undone, I argued. So many things that I still need to do. So many fences to mend. I hadn't said I love you to those I care about. It didn't matter. I had to leave anyway.

She took me by the hand, and as we drifted upward, I looked down at my rumpled bed and all of the pill bottles and other evidence of a prolonged illness. It felt good to be so weightless, so pain free, so unrestricted from the confines of my sickly body. But wait, I hadn't gone anywhere for a very long time. I was really too frail to travel. It didn't matter. I went anyway.

Of course I will be missed by some. Family and friends will mourn for a while. That is the natural order of things. That is the way it has always been. But after a time, thoughts of me will grow dim.

Oh sure, my name will come up on occasion. But only to comment about the good or the bad. Things that happen in the middle are never remembered. But that's OK. They didn't matter anyway.

So how will you be remembered? And who will come for you? Are you ready for such a visitor? Is your house in order? Have you at least swept the floor? We put a lot of time and effort into maintaining the "structure" that we have lived in for so many years. It is difficult to give it up without an argument. But it doesn't really matter. It was only a rental anyway.

I'm not ready.
I'm not sure I'll ever be.
But I'll prepare how best I can
When the angel comes for me.

This one came to me after attending the funeral of a friend. Grief is always lessened by the knowledge that there is something better awaiting us on the other side, and the belief that someone is waiting to guide us through that golden door.

I'VE GONE ON AHEAD

When all thoughts of me have gone
And I no longer fill your mind
And the future plans we made
All have faded with the time

Perhaps sometimes you'll think of me
And of the things I'd say
How I would love you endlessly
Until my dying day

You opened up my eyes to love
You filled my heart with pleasure
The moments that we had, my dear
Are memories I'll treasure

So just because you may forget
I've pledged my love so true
I'll keep your memories alive
With constant thoughts of you

And when it's time for you to go
To leave this time-bound plain
Be not afraid to enter there
I'll shield you from all pain

I'll save for you a place my dear
Where we'll always be together
Where love will flourish every day
And we'll be bound forever

I know we'll be together then
As our love was meant to be
There'll be no need to rush my dear
For you'll be there with me

When I go first don't grieve for me
Be happy and be free
For I've just gone to prepare for us
A place in eternity

Many stories have been told
Of those who've gone before
A loved one will be waiting there
Beside that golden door

This poem, as with many others, came to me as I awoke in the early morning. The words came to me faster than I could write them down. My thought was that people are capable of so much more than they think they are. They often look elsewhere for inspiration when everything they need is within themselves.

JUST ANOTHER FISH STORY

I sat beside a stream one day just to ease my weary mind.
My line was in the water, but my reel wouldn't wind.
A half-broke pole, I thought, was just the thing for me to use,
For I didn't want to catch. My intention was to snooze.

So I leaned back on my elbows and I gazed towards the sky,
As I listened to a songbird and the buzzing of a fly.
A gentle breeze was blowing and a perfume filled the air,
For the flowers that were near me boasted blooms beyond compare.

I had left the busy city where the traffic never slows,
And I came up to this quiet place where the water gently flows.
I thought if I could fish a while then maybe I would find
A place somewhere within myself to bring me peace of mind.

When suddenly my pole lurched and gave me quite a start.
I first reached for my pole, and then reached for my heart.
I knew I'd caught a fighter though I never really tried.
I wondered, would it be best baked, or taste best crisply fried?

I struggled with the frightened fish, but I finally pulled him in.
Then I stood there in amazement at the sight of such a win.
I had never seen a fish like that and I marveled at the sight.
His colors were of such a hue, they could surely light the night.

There was white, pink, orange and gold, and many shades of blue.
Green, brown, black and red, and there was purple too.
This can't be real for nothing could have colors such as this.
But here they were before me, and all were on a fish.

Then suddenly some words exploded from the fish's mouth.
"You caught me fair and square," he said, "as I was swimming south."
I couldn't speak. What could I say? Am I mistaken in what I hear?
Fish can't talk. That's what they say, but here is one quite near.

"Yes, I can talk, and I can hear, and I can see you very well.
So here's the deal, if you agree, and promise not to tell.
My freedom for a promise kept, and I will show you how,
To be the man you want to be, and you can start right now."

It took a while to accept the fact that a fish had talked to me.
And I could understand him just as clearly as can be.
But finally I listened to the words he chose so well,
And agreed to keep his secret, and never would I tell.

The fish said he would take me to a place where I would meet,
Someone who knew just what it took to get me on my feet.
He said that I could see this man and look him in the eye,
That he would give me all the tools to live before I die.

So off we went on a southerly course to see the man who knows
Just what it takes to live a life with confidence that flows.
The fish swam fast along the bank and I walked fast as well.
My thoughts on things I would finally know, but things I could never tell.

The path that I was taking, I had never seen before.
It meandered through a meadow, but was never far from shore.
Flowers rare in beauty lined the pathway where I walked,
As my mind raced through the day's events, and the fact a fish had talked.

When I was about to give up hope that we would reach the place,
Where I would find the man who knew where I'd find peace and grace,
We came upon a whirling pool that glistened in the sun.
The surface like a mirror where the waters slowly run.

I asked the fish, "Where is this man who knows just what I need?
For I see no one here. I think you snookered me indeed."
The fish said, "You're a foolish man to think that I would cheat.
I told you that you caught me fair, and that I had been beat.

"I said I'd show you someone who has answers that you seek,
Who knows you can't be strong, without also being weak.
Now I have brought you to someone who knows just how to live,
Who knows the art of when to take and also when to give.

"So look into the pool my friend and you will plainly see,
The one who will impart to you, just who you need to be.
Look deeply into that man's soul and you will understand,
That the figure in the water is the same one on the land."

I knew my mind was playing tricks
To think a fish could talk.
What next I thought sarcastically,
To find the fish could walk?

"A trick it is, you played on me,
For there is no one that I see,
Except the reflection of my face,
And no one else to take its place."

The fish responded knowingly,
"It's within yourself to set you free.
Look inward when you want to see.
Don't look to others, or fish like me.

You have the tools to be a better man
And face the troubles from which you ran.
So formulate a simple plan
And carry it out as I know you can."

I calmed my thoughts and began to think
About a life that was on the brink
Of ending up in a tangled mess,
Of things I've done much too excess.

As I gazed into the swirling pool,
I began to think me less a fool.
For I realized the fish was right.
I can run away or stand and fight.

So I began to understand
That those live best who lend a hand.
That I must be a better man
And do some good while I still can.

So I kept this tale all to myself,
Back in my mind upon a shelf.
For never would I tell, you see,
That I met a fish much smarter than me.

Many have lost more trying to win more. This can be said for time, love, prestige, power, and many other things besides money.

LADY LUCK

Seems I'm always chasing Lady Luck
I'll soon run out of time
Thought I'd spend a dime to make a buck,
But I spent a buck just to make a dime

What is this thing called luck, you ask,
That's always so elusive?
Why does it take me to the task,
And treat me so abusive?

The secret seems forever lost
How best to earn some bread
I've used my hands at some great cost
More often than my head

So if you spend your waking hours
For Lady Luck to call
And fate forever keeps your powers
Behind the old eight ball

Take my advice and give it up
Don't bend until you break it
No outside force will fill your cup
Luck is only what you make it

I awoke one morning from a dream in which I saw a beautiful but lonely flower on a hill. A bed of lesser flowers seemed to look up from their plot below. That seems to be the way of life for many. Who we want and what we want is sometimes out of reach. Thus, this poem.

LILLY

Lilly was a flower growing high upon a hill.
Sweet William was a flower down below.
Her mantle glowing halo-white with golden-yellow frill.
While he was clad in purple with some shades of blue to show.

Ever since he grew enough to peak above the grass,
He yearned to stand beside her high above.
If he could just get close enough to touch the lovely lass,
He'd tell her of his sweet undying love.

He marveled at her beauty and the way she held her head.
Her slender body weaving in the gentle summer breeze.
The fragrance of her perfume wafted through the flower bed.
And to everyone around her it did please.

Her regal bearing signified a status far above
The poor and ragged flowers down below.
And there was nothing he could do to ever show his love
To the beauty that he'd never come to know.

If he could just be by her side, he'd never ask for more.
He'd be happy just to know that she was near.
But he was destined to a life that many would deplore.
Since mistaken for a weed was constant fear.

But wishes never make things happen as we want them to.
No matter how we try to make them real.
For he was fixed in place and there was nothing he could do.
He'd never know the kiss he planned to steal.

He would gladly give his life if even once before he died,
He could show her all the love that he would pour,
Upon the ageless beauty who would never be denied.
Her slightest wish would never be a chore.

Is it fate that sets a stately princess high upon a hill,
While a lowly serf is stationed far below?
Just to see and never touch your love is such a bitter pill
To a longing heart that suffers such a blow.

But in time all flowers were reduced to brown and tangled weeds.
And no longer would they grace the fertile fields.
And fate is often fickle with our wishes and our needs.
For a mower soon did slay the bounteous yields.

All the words Sweet William uttered never seemed to make it through.
Months of longing to be with Lilly come what may.
Yet in the final outcome, all his wishes did come true.
For they finally are together in the landfill where they lay.

(I originally ended this poem here,
but my wife and daughter wanted a happier ending.
So I added the following stanzas)

For things that seem so final, lover's prayers will often bring
Miracles that harken to the angel's call.
Fields of flowers once more surfaced with the gentle rains of spring.
Rising from the seeds left over from the fall.

But the hill that held a Lilly looking down upon the rest
Was now laden with a deep and flowing grass.
Where the little chipmunks scurry and the timid quail nest.
And no longer stood the Lilly that had graced the field with class.

Far down the hill where flowers grow that never get much care,
Are two lovers all aglow when the light grows dim.
For a Lilly fair with mantel white and Sweet William huddle there.
Since he couldn't come to her, she had come to him.

I was searching for my glasses one day, and though I searched all of the places I normally put them, they were nowhere to be found. I stopped to scratch my head as I contemplated my next move. That's when I discovered them. They were on my head.

LOST

I lost something important yesterday
As important as a memory can be
But I cannot remember, try as I might
If it was important to me

It was gone in less than a blink
My mind is in disarray
It must have been my ability to think,
For my thoughts have flown away

I've searched my entire memory bank
My thinking all laid bare
They say it's just old age to thank
For nothing left up there

I think I've finally broken through
As things are coming back
But there isn't much that I can do
To keep my thoughts on track

I've finally discovered what I've lost
It's something I'll never find
And it all came at a very dear cost
For I've finally lost my mind

Is it fate that determines who will be a cop and who will be a crook? Some say it's the environment, while others blame the upbringing. I've known people who seem destined for a life of crime, but turn out to be upstanding citizens. The opposite can be said of some who start out on a golden path, but for some reason end up on a muddy road. Is the kind of life we lead already determined? Is it already written in "The Book?"

MY FATE: A CRIMINAL'S TALE

I learned to take at an early age.
My father taught me so.
I busted from my darkened cage,
With a ball and chain in tow.

What wasn't given, I would take.
I'd learned it as a child.
There were no boundaries they could make
For those who were born so wild.

I once had dreams of a better life.
Dreams I could not fulfill.
So I took them with a gun and knife,
While high on drink and pill.

I took and took and never gave.
Like my father taught me to.
My path through life was mine to pave,
Until my life was through.

And then, one night, with gun in hand,
I made my last mistake.
The man in blue would take a stand,
I'm bound for the Reaper's wake.

On this hard slab I'm lying still.
Reserved only for the dead.
I finally took and took until,
I took a bullet to the head.

They said my fate was yet to be,
On that December morn.
But that's not how it was, you see.
My fate was determined the day I was born.

MY FATE: A COP'S TALE

I learned to give at an early age.
My father taught me so
He wore the badge of courage,
So that everyone would know.

The man in blue was always there
With a lesson and a rule.
His guidelines were so very clear.
Don't cheat or play the fool.

Look not to others to guide you on.
Just look within your soul.
For you are not the devil's pawn.
Public service is your goal.

So I took up my father's call
To do the job I should.
For others I would give my all,
And do the best I could

I daily practiced his advice.
Don't take when you can give.
And never trust the rolling dice
On what it takes to live.

My duties took me to a place,
I didn't want to go.
I met a gunman face to face,
And I dealt the fatal blow.

They said my fate was yet to be
On that December morn.
But that's not how it was, you see.
My fate was determined the day I was born.

I wrote this for my sister, Annie. I sent it to her for her birthday. She died a few months later. The pastor read it at her funeral and then placed the copy in her coffin. It was buried with her. I was very shy when I started school. Bigger kids used to pick on me until Annie wrestled them to the ground. After that, they left me alone. She always sang country songs while we were milking the cows. She had a beautiful voice. I still miss her.

MY SISTER ANNIE AND ME

She was born in April on an Iowa farm,
My sister Annie with her natural charm.
One of thirteen kids who would work each day
Raising corn and beans and oats and hay.

As her younger brother, I soon would see
That my sister Annie was looking out for me.
She fought the kids who ruined my day.
She would take them down and make them pay.

She could be tough as nails or soft as silk.
She could coax the cows to give more milk.
She would sing them a song that would soothe the herd.
Her voice was as sweet as a young songbird.

Many years have passed since those childhood days
And we both have changed in many ways.
But my sister Annie will always be,
In my heart, in my thoughts, and dear to me.

Now when our life will cease to be.
And it's time to go for Annie and me.
And we stand before the Pearly Gates
For permission to enter those Grand Estates,

Then Annie will take me by the hand
And lead me to that Promised Land.
And tell the Angels she'll look out for me,
Just as she's done since she was three.

Yes, she will speak for me again.
And ask them please to let me in.
And the Angels, they will all agree
To let me in, because of my sister An-nie.

A man is truly blessed to have a sister. I was very fortunate. I had five. All were very dear to me in one way or another. My sister, Annie, however, seemed to be the one who always came to my defense. But then, she was always the first one to offer assistance to anyone in need. We need more Annies in this world.

This is another poem inspired by a funeral that I attended. It was a somber occasion, but there was a spirit present that transcended death and sorrow. A peaceful feeling seemed to fill the air. I attempted to capture the mood in this poem.

MY SPIRIT SHALL REMAIN

The mournful sound of the church bells toll
Across the valley floor
And echo up the mountain side
'Till the sound is heard no more

Inside the church where the organ plays
A young man's eyes are closed
His hands are clasped across his chest
And a rose beside him posed

The woman standing by his side
Fights back a falling tear
Her veil concealing grief so great
More pain than she can bear

A love they'd known when he once lived
Transcends the foul of death
For even now he calls to her
As he did with his last breath

The lonely figure standing there
As they lay him in the ground
Remained as if to speak with him
When no one was around

He'd promised her he'd never leave
He'd never go away
But now he's left her all alone
Oh, what a lonely day

She didn't know just what to do
She didn't want to live
If he could not give up his death
Then she her life would give

As she was standing all alone
She felt his presence there
She felt a kiss upon her cheek
His fingers through her hair

My love, he whispered in her ear
I said I'd never go
My spirit shall remain with you
Though my body rests below

The rose that once beside him lay
Was suddenly in her hair
And a gentle breeze brushed softly by
To caress her skin so fair

A smile came slowly to her face
For now at peace was she
Her love would be there evermore
Throughout eternity.

The older I get, the more my mind drifts back to those early days on the family farm in Iowa. Even as a child, I realized how fortunate I was to have been born on a farm. I mean that in a literal sense. My father delivered me on the dining room table during a blinding snowstorm.

I would be working in the fields, dog tired physically, but feeling so good emotionally that I felt sorry for all the kids living in town who weren't able to enjoy the life of a farmer.

Throughout my life, there always seemed to be one more furrow to plow.

ONE MORE FURROW TO PLOW

Giddy up, Queenie. C'mon Prince.
We're tired, but we can't quit now.
We started early and we haven't stopped since,
But we've one more furrow to plow.

The rows get longer as the day goes by.
It's hard and you want to quit now.
But we've gotta keep going and not ask why,
For we've one more furrow to plow.

First plow the fields, then disk and drag.
Gotta get the ground ready now.
For it's late in the season and the planting can't lag.
So we've one more furrow to plow.

I know you're worn, and I'm worn too,
But we've gotta keep going somehow.
It won't be long until we're through,
But we've one more furrow to plow.

When my final sun sets and the stars are lit,
And the Angels come to take me now,
I'll ask my Lord, "Can you wait a bit?"
For I've one more furrow to plow.

Several years ago, I went to the IRS building to obtain some information for a project that I was working on. It was a sobering experience. Desperate and pathetic looking people were lined up at the windows sorting through documents that they hoped would diminish their tax burden. Some were in such terrible physical condition, I was concerned they wouldn't live to fulfill their mission. For some reason, the scene reminded me of rows of headstones, where in the end, the wealthy and the poor all end up the same. I returned home and scribbled out this poem.

ROW ON ROW

God planted seeds
And watched them grow
In His Garden
Row on row.

Some ground was rich
And some was poor.
Some plants would wilt
And some would soar.

Some said the climate
Was to blame
For causing those
To come up lame.

While others said,
It's their own choice
To surge ahead
Or give no voice.

But I believe
That each is meant
To do the things
That Heaven sent.

For God assigns us
To A task
Even though
We didn't ask.

But earthly life
Will surely end
And any wrong
We must amend.

We will return
Just as before
When we were waiting
At the door.

The stones and urns
Stand in a line,
With grass and flowers,
And trees of pine.

And there we are
Six feet below,
Where once again
We're row on row.

It has been said that death is the great equalizer. Some complain, however, that even in death, the more affluent still stand out with their marble headstones and their brass-plated plaques. But beneath all of the tapestries of fortune and fame, everyone becomes the same.

I had a friend who often reminded me of the nature of things when something didn't turn out as expected. "Sometimes you eat the bear, and sometimes the bear eats you," he would say. I sometimes used these exact words after apprehending a burglar. It kept rolling around in my head until I decided to put it to verse.

SOMETIMES THE HUNTER.
SOMETIMES THE PREY.

A man sat silently in the dark,
With no excuse to give
For failing to understand the rule
You have to die before you can live

He spent his life collecting things
He really didn't need
And all the problems wanting brings
Led him to a devilish deed

He was a hunter of the night
He took without a thought
With no concern for another's plight
Nor sorry for the hell he wrought

Things looked so simple when he was young
He thought his life was right on track
The road was narrow, straight and true
He'd reach his goal and not look back

But things never seem to happen
As we like to think they will
Seems they often catch us nappin'
And not prepared for the final hill

But fate has a way of thwarting wants
For needs are often what hold sway
He hadn't considered the facts of life
Sometimes the hunter. Sometimes the prey

Just like the animals, we all become hunters and we all become prey in one form or another. Life is a balancing act. The art of survival is to not stray too far from the center.

Many of us dream of things that in real life could never be. Our dreams seem to vanish with the wind. But sometimes, reality becomes even more rewarding than we could have ever dreamed.

STREAMS OF LIFE

It seems that many a person's dreams
Just end up in disaster.
But in this world of negative streams
The positive streams flow faster

The rocks from which disaster sprung
Are now as smooth as gems
I've stepped up from the bottom rung
And snipped the flower's stems

I wrote this one for my granddaughter who was studying the Fifth Amendment:

THE FIFTH AMENDMENT

The Fifth Amendment cites the rule
Of self-incrimination.
It's just another legal tool
That forms our education.

When there's concern that what you say
Might cause you legal grief,
Your testimony can't be forced,
If you will just be brief.

No need to lie or shade the truth.
No explanation needed,
As long as you are careful,
And the Fifth Amendment heeded

So when your mother asks you
About the boy she saw you with,
Just tell her, I am sorry mom,
But I must plead the Fifth.

Love can be a one-sided and fleeting thing that leaves a person feeling empty and confused. It can also be so breathtakingly beautiful, so spiritual and so complete, it could only have come from Heaven. This is the story of a love that knows no bounds.

THE HEAVY HAND OF FATE

I ran my fingers through her hair
As she lay by my side.
My feelings for her all laid bare
There was nothing left to hide

I loved her from the very first,
And she in turn loved me.
But like a bubble that has burst,
No longer can it be.

Our hearts entwined in a single weave
Must now be torn apart.
I never thought that she would leave.
And break my aging heart.

I begged her at least a thousand times,
Don't leave me here like this.
For as surely as the church bell chimes,
Her loving touch I'll miss.

Regardless of my somber mood,
Her love had never wavered.
And even with my manners rude,
I was still the one she favored.

But the time has come for her to go,
To leave this earthly realm.
The timing isn't mine to know,
For fate is at the helm.

I've known the heavy hand of fate.
I've felt her stinging blows.
But this one is the worst of late.
The heartbreak never slows.

I know not where our future lies,
But one thing is for certain.
True love still burned within her
As fate drew the final curtain.

I mourn the day she slipped away.
It was very hard to leave her.
And I will pine away each day.
For my beautiful Golden Retriever.

Funny thing about love. It is more than a feeling. It transcends the bounds that we humans place on everything. It becomes the air that we breathe and the nourishment for our bodies. Thank God for love.

I was preparing to shave one morning when I was startled by what I saw in the mirror. I was used to seeing the image of a farm boy, tan and strong and wide eyed with enthusiasm in anticipation of another beautiful day. How did I age so suddenly? How did I suddenly become a bystander to my own life? Where did the years go? How could I have missed the transition from youth to old age? All of these questions ran through my mind as I tried to reconcile a barefoot kid suddenly becoming an old man.

THE OLD MAN

I wonder who that
Old man can be?
The one in the mirror
Staring back at me?

I've never seen
That face before.
It's old and wrinkled
With lines galore.

His bushy brows
Nearly cover his eyes.
Perhaps he's wearing
A clever disguise.

His hair is white
And he needs a shave.
There was sadness in
The stare he gave.

His eyes are dim
And watered down.
And his brow is frozen
Into a frown.

What happened to
The man I knew?
The one who many
A dragon slew?

The one who used
To smile at me,
When a reflection of
His face I'd see?

The one in youth
Who was very bold?
And could never imagine
Growing old?

Once mighty limbs
Are feeble now.
To Old Father Time,
He is forced to bow.

It seems like only
Yesterday,
When all he had to do
Was play.

And now his life
Is at an end.
And any wrong
He must amend.

For in the place
That he will know.
And where we all
Still wish to go,

Judgment is there
For all to face,
And nothing else
To take its place.

So, do some good.
Don't tempt your fate.
For one more day
May be too late.

In our desire for perfection, we often pass up opportunities that we would gladly have settled for had we realized that our vision of perfection was not based on reality. If you are searching for perfection, you are usually looking in the wrong place.

THE PERFECT MAN

Two men on a park bench resting.
"Are you married, if I may ask?"
"No," said the other jesting.
"I've never been up to the task."

I'm really not opposed to marriage,
But I've seen others take the fall.
And I know I shouldn't disparage,
But there are pitfalls to it all.

So I decided to take my time
In search of the perfect mate.
I'd find the one with love sublime,
And not be spurned on our first date.

But years went by and there was never
One who filled the total bill.
In my search I did endeavor
To find the one who'd love me still.

And then one day I finally found her.
She was perfect in every way.
My search for love was finally over.
I'd marry her without delay.

One moonlit night in a horse and carriage,
On bended knee I proposed my plan.
But she refused my hand in marriage.
For she was looking for the perfect man.

Perfection is something we all strive for, but never truly obtain. Many have sacrificed a good life while searching fruitlessly for a great life. Looking for perfection in a relationship is like fishing when you are starving. It is best not to throw back the fish you caught in the hopes of catching a bigger one. Maybe the stream you are fishing in has been fished out, or it was never deep enough to contain the trophy-size fish you are looking for. Then there is always the possibility that you will catch a real beauty. But it may be inedible.

I realized I was getting old one day when I attempted to do something that was once effortless, but now took a great deal of effort. Where did my youth go? It seemed to have disappeared over night. This one is from my aging mind.

THE SETTING SUN

The sun is sinking in the west
The cattle are bedded down
The dove is nestled in her nest
And the leaves are turning brown

The corn is standing in the field
The ears are hanging low
And we must harvest all they yield
Before the coming snow

There was a time when things were new
And all about was wonder
When grass was cradled by the dew
And a serenade of thunder

Seasons liken to my life
From spring to winter's pall
And after summer's drum and fife
I'll heed the Master's call

Each part has played a defining role
A beginning and an end
That left a marker on my soul
And a willing knee to bend

It took me years to realize
That time is ever fleeting
It left so bare the thin disguise
Of a heart no longer beating

Where did the time I wasted go?
Why wasn't I aware?
Of everything I was destined for
With the life I had to share

Where once a euphoric feeling dwelled
Resides a checkered past
It matters not all things rebelled
My time has come at last

The winter of my life is here
No time is left for sorrow
And there is nothing more to fear
For I've seen my last tomorrow

I am reaching the age in my life when the sun has settled below the horizon and the light is dimming. But just as I looked back at the end of a busy day in the fields of the family farm, and felt a sense of accomplishment in reaping what I have sown, so too do I look back upon my life. I have been blessed with a long and fruitful life. A person cannot ask for more than that.

I think many of us have failed to answer the door because we didn't recognize the knock. It is understandable. We have too much to do. We don't want to waste our precious time on a stranger who, more likely than not, wants something from us instead of give something to us. Sometimes we answer the door, but fail to recognize who we are turning away. I have experienced that scenario. Maybe you have, too.

THE STRANGER AT MY DOOR

I heard her knocking at my door.
But I was busy inside.
She'd come to visit many times before.
But her entry I'd denied.

I didn't know her anyway,
So why should I waste my time?
I wasn't giving up my day.
Or spending another dime.

For she surely wanted something,
As people always do.
So whenever I hear the doorbell ring,
It's to ply their wares anew.

I failed to recognize her,
As she comes in many a disguise.
She thought she had me fooled.
But I was twice as wise.

I finally opened up the door,
Intent to have my say.
But I needn't worry anymore.
Opportunity had gone away.

The routine of things sometimes makes us complacent. We tend to put things off with thoughts that there is always a tomorrow. We have plenty of time. The end is so very far away. Until suddenly, it's upon us, and here to stay.

THE SUN CAME UP AGAIN TODAY

The sun came up again today,
Just as it did the day before.
It didn't know I'd gone away,
Awaiting entry at Heaven's door.

This frail body once was strong.
The end was oh so far away.
I waited for it, oh, so long.
Now, suddenly, it's here to stay.

When I was a kid, I couldn't imagine growing old. Thirty-five seemed to be the magic number. I couldn't visualize living longer than that. Now that I am nearing the end, I often think of those days. I have been blessed with a long life and many happy memories. This poem pretty much sums up my thoughts:

TIME

The wondrous days of yesteryear go coursing through my mind.
Conveying thoughts of days and nights that I have left behind.
I reminisce and sort out thoughts which help to pass the hour.
And in the end I find my thoughts are far more sweet than sour.

When young, the thought of growing old was hard to visualize.
I knew that I would never reach the age of thirty five.
The future seemed so far away and time was ever slow.
My longing took me everywhere without the means to go.

I thought that things would never change, the way they were, they'd stay.
I thought that all my loved ones would never go away.
All things familiar to me then, and which I loved so much,
Would always be there for me, to just reach out and touch.

The years passed very slowly then, but pass indeed they did.
Until I shed the thoughts that are the hallmark of a kid.
The age was near when long ago I thought I would be dead.
But here I was with children and a wife a long time wed.

What makes a man escape the child, but still have childish thought?
To believe that he is capable of winning all wars fought?
It must be part of middle age and confidence it breeds.
Long since sowing wild oats and all the other seeds.

Then comes the time when middle age seems like so long ago.
When once more life is filled with dreams that thru the mind do flow.
What wondrous magic time can do to ease the troubled mind.
For in the later years of life, the thoughts of life grow kind.

Forgotten are the days of anguish, all the grief and strife.
As though a master surgeon chose to excise with a knife.
And in their place the many thoughts that gathered thru the miles,
Have all turned in to special dreams of sunny days and smiles.

Time seemed to drag by as a child. But the older I get, the faster time seems to fly. I try not to dwell on the many mistakes I have made and the heartaches I have caused. I wasted enough time doing them. I'll waste no more time thinking about them. At least that is what I tell myself. But they still take up too much of my valuable time.

We make so many promises we seldom keep. A promise should be treated like a loaded gun. It may be meaningless to the person issuing it, but to the receiver it is as relevant as a bullet in the breech of a gun. Once fired, it can't be called back. No indiscriminate shooting. Judge the distance and make sure you are capable of hitting the target before placing a bullet in the chamber. This poem is a reminder of the importance of following through on a promise. A friend took this poem to his pastor who used it to preach the entire services one Sunday morning.

TOMORROW

I promised to call tomorrow
For I had much to do today.
But as so often happens
The days just slipped away.

I'll visit her tomorrow.
Just one more day I thought.
My mother wouldn't mind
If some extra time I bought.

But when I came to visit
Friends were there to visit too.
She was dressed-up in her finest
All laid out for us to view.

A promise may be solemn
As a bullet in the breech.
But the trouble with tomorrow is,
It's always out of reach.

I called upon a long-time friend
Who had recently lost his job.
He once was filled with laughter,
But all he did was sob.

There was nothing that he wanted,
Except listen to his woes.
But other things were on my mind.
And so life's story goes.

I'll call again tomorrow.
To that promise he had clung.
But that night the Angels took him
From the closet where he hung.

A promise may be solemn
As a bullet in the breech.
But the trouble with tomorrow is,
It's always out of reach.

"Repent your sins," the pastor said,
At Service Sunday morn.
I'd heard the same words spoken
Since the day that I was born.

Of course I will, I promised.
I've time enough for that.
I knew I should have heeded,
But the words had fallen flat.

How did the years slip by so fast?
I'll repent my sins tomorrow.
But that night the angels came for me.
No time was left to borrow.

A promise may be solemn
As a bullet in the breech.
But the trouble with tomorrow is,
It's always out of reach.

So if your obligations
Run counter to your plan.
And you are forced to now confront
The things from which you ran.

And you are thinking, as I thought,
What difference can it make?
For it will be as simple
As a thirst that I can slake.

Don't make an empty promise,
As I have often done.
Or waste the precious moments
Of a life that's so hard won.

For your promise may be solemn
As a bullet in the breech.
But the trouble with tomorrow is,
It's always out of reach.

What if you were able to relive yesterday? What changes would you make? What would you do differently? Maybe it isn't too late. Today will soon be yesterday. Consider what you will think tomorrow and make the necessary changes today.

While she would, no doubt, correct me on my punctuation and diction, I dedicate this poem to Mrs. Irene Heine, my high school English teacher in Denver, Iowa in 1952; to the principal, Mr. Pinkerton, whose policy was to require no homework assignments as farm boys were too busy to be saddled with homework; and to teachers everywhere, whose worth far surpass the recognition they receive for the important job they do. I was unable to attend our 50th class reunion, so I sent this poem instead.

TRIBUTE TO DENVER HIGH

The memories that flood my mind
As time goes passing by,
Forever seem to center on
My days at Denver High.

We studied literary works back then,
By Shelley, Keats and Nelly Bly
Exposed to influence of the pen,
An integral part of Denver High.

Of all the lessons I have learned
The one on which I can rely
Is that no friendship will be spurned
Whose origin was Denver High.

There were differences among us,
In our values and our tastes,
But the common bond among us
Was that we were all classmates.

So I say to all my classmates
Who are gathered on this day,
And to those who've gone before us,
Who are better off, I pray,

I am better having known you,
And I miss the good old days,
When I worked and played among you,
Learned your language and your ways.

The many years that span the time
Since graduation day,
Can't dim the memories sublime
Or disturb them where they lay.

There are those who pride in winning wars
Or conquering the sky.
But I'm proud to be a graduate
Of good old Denver High.

I often look back with fondness on my days at Denver High School. I missed the first two weeks of my freshman year because we were threshing oats and every hand was needed. The first two years were difficult as we lived five miles away and I had to scramble for transportation. I was relieved during my junior and senior year when the bus came by the door. Our class put on a school play both years. I had no intention of participating, but Mrs. Heine made everyone try out for each part and I ended up with the lead male part both years. What a wonderful time that was. Maybe it has become so memorable because I got to kiss the girl in both plays.

I wrote this after another police officer was killed in the line of duty. We often question why God would take someone who is doing good deeds while the bad ones seem to linger. But after careful consideration, I compare it to the selection process of sports teams. They always take the best players first and leave the worst for last. Maybe God has the same priorities.

WE LOST ANOTHER GOOD MAN TODAY

We lost another good man today.
Cut down in the prime of his life.
He's gone to a better world, I pray.
But he left behind two kids and a wife.

I've often asked, why take the best?
Why not someone who matters less?
But I've finally put that question to rest.
For it could be me, I must confess.

But then I stopped to think things through.
That's not the way things work in life.
For the cycle will begin anew.
With peace there always comes some strife.

Just stop to think what the sports teams do.
The last selected perform the worst.
The very best are the very few.
And the best are always taken first.

As a Phoenix police polygraph examiner and interrogator for more than six years, and thousands of examinations conducted, I've heard just about every horrible thing that one person can possibly do to another. Sometimes, I would have to run to the restroom in the middle of an interrogation and vomit. I would then return and finish the interrogation. Hearing so much vile stuff hour after hour, day after day was more than my mind was capable of digesting. It was as if I had eaten too much and my stomach rebelled. In this case, however, it was my mind that was rebelling.

WHAT DOES A POLYGRAPH EXAMINER DO?

What does a polygraph examiner do
With all of the stuff he has heard?
With all of the hideous things, unspeakable things
That he must never divulge and can never dispose of?

What does a polygraph examiner do
With the mournful cries of sorrow and remorse?
With the pitiful cries of justice and injustice?
With faults and blames and just plain trash?

What does a polygraph examiner do
With all of that stored up information?
With all of that rotting, stinking mass of verbal garbage
That he must carry with him from the moment of inception?

What does a polygraph examiner do
With all of the tears and sorrow?
With all of the admissions and confessions,
Explanations and concessions?

He puts it all in his little bag
That occupies the deepest vault in his mind.
One that is tied with an unbreakable string.
And takes it with him to the grave

I've often wondered about the possibility of a past life. It seems the only explanation when a four year old can play the piano like a professional, or paint a Rembrandt or a Picasso like the old masters.

WHEN I COME AROUND AGAIN

I've been here many times before.
But not who I am today.
I've been many different people
Who were never meant to stay

There are many lives within me
That I've garnered through the years.
Some were filled with laughter,
And some were filled with tears

I've been high and I've been low.
Many faces I have known.
Each has played a salient part.
But only one is shown.

From the dusty plains of Africa
To the rains of Ranchipur.
It's hard to tell from whence I came.
But I've been here before.

From the gold-clad mansions of a rich man's dreams
To the slums of the poorest poor.
I may have known them both, you see,
Because I've been here before.

I may have been the master,
Or a sailor far from shore.
I may have been a lowly slave.
But I've been here before.

There were times when life was but a jest.
Where I played fast and loose.
I may have faced the pirate's knife.
Or known the hangman's noose.

I may have been a warrior.
The bravest of the brave.
Or I may have been a beggar.
Or even a gnarly knave.

Or born into royalty.
A king or a queen.
Or the hated executioner,
With his cleaver sharpened keen.

A blacksmith, maybe.
Or a field hand.
Or maybe a gentleman
With acres of land.

I may have been a doctor,
Who cured the very sick.
Or maybe I was a mason,
Who laid the building's brick.

I don't recall just where or when
I've trod this earthly realm.
Or every sea I've sailed in life
While I've been at the helm.

But each has worked to shape me
Into what I've come to be.
Yet it may take generations
Before I'll learn to see.

I'm someone who I sometimes were,
And someone who I've always been.
And the cycle will begin anew
When I come around again.

I wrote this one after standing in line at a grocery store and reading a tabloid about a man who won over three-hundred-million dollars in the lottery. His comment was, "Now I can buy the helicopter that I was considering whether to buy or not." He was already wealthy. My first thought was why someone who has so much, easily gets more. Then I realized how fortunate I was compared to so many others. So, I put my thoughts on paper.

WHEN IS IT GOING TO BE MY TURN?

I stood in line at the grocery store.
People in front with so much more.
I looked around, all checkouts full.
Some pushing one cart while another they'd pull.

Then I read where the lottery was won by a man
Who already had money and acres of land.
But here he was with money to burn,
While the lottery angels to me did spurn.

I watched as others were promoted ahead.
From time of their birth, they were always spoon-fed.
And someone had always paved their way.
From this golden path they didn't stray.

And I asked of fate, please let me learn.
When is it going to be...my turn?

There are times when I cry, "Oh! Woe is me!"
From so much strife I am seldom free.
It always seems that others get by
Without a strain or a tear in their eye.

So, I decided to look around,
While I kept my feet on solid ground.
I would try to compare my life to theirs,
And see how each have earned their shares.

Then I thought of the line that I often see.
They too wanted food, but it didn't include me.
For those were the people at a charity bank.
And I thought to myself, I have God to thank.

And I asked of fate, will I still learn?
Is it coming for me? Must I take...my turn?

My neighbor lost his house today.
Without a job, he couldn't pay.
A foreclosure sign stands in the yard.
Just to see it there is awful hard.

Then I strolled on down to the city park,
Just to spend some time, about an hour before dark.
I saw a family underneath a tree.
I was staring at them and they were looking at me.

I watched as they all made ready for bed.
On the cold hard ground they would lay their head.
A mother and father and children too.
There was nothing else that they could do.

And I asked of fate, will I still learn?
Is it coming for me? Must I take...my turn?

I went to the hospital to visit a friend.
I could see he was close to reaching the end.
I sat by his side as his eyes grew dim.
And I thought to myself, thank God I'm not him.

I watched my friend be buried today.
In a very deep grave, surrounded by clay.
He didn't have much, not many to mourn.
It had been that way since the day he was born.

I saw a mother weep today
For a child who recently passed away.
They pulled him from a swimming pool.
I watched in silence and I thought, how cruel.

And I asked of fate, please let me learn,
Who am I to have missed...my turn?

I went down town to the poorest part
Where a homeless man was pushing his cart.
Where soup kitchens feed the down and out,
And something to eat is always in doubt.

Where the hungry and desperate on the sidewalks lie.
Some barely living, some ready to die.
While people walk by without even a glance.
Never having experienced a life of chance.

A father and mother and children too.
Hungry and thirsty with nothing to do.
No home and no food are the problems they face.
I was glad I never was in their place.

And I asked of fate, please let me learn,
Is it coming for me, or did I miss...my turn?

I am dressed in my finest. Good is said about me.
I am resting on satin as smooth as can be.
The flowers abound, roses, lilies and more.
So many they cover the whole carpet floor.

Now, finally, I am where I asked when I'd be,
Leading the procession with all eyes on me.
With followers stretching for miles on end.
Cars with their lights on, and all for a friend.

My time is now here when they're coming for me.
For a place they've prepared, underneath an oak tree.
And there I will rest for all eternity.
No longer to wonder when it's going to be...my turn.

It is finally...my turn.

Our barn looks old, weathered, and lonely. It has passed its period of usefulness. It seems to reflect the feelings of many as we age. There are times when we feel sorry for ourselves. Maybe we didn't reach our full potential as we see it. There are always so many things left undone. Time has passed us by. This poem sums up those thoughts.

WHO AM I?

Sometimes I cry for no reason.
Oh, they are not droplets that show.
They are just tears of the season.
Not precursors to long tales of woe.

Yes, they are just watered down versions
Of dreams that I longed to fulfill.
Thoughts that are now just diversions
From memories that bother me still.

There were so many things I had planned.
As others so often do.
I was destined for a life more grand.
It was something that I always knew.

But who am I to set my sight
On something I could never see?
And who am I to think I might
Be someone I could never be?

Life can be ever so grand,
Or something that misery holds.
It depends on the law of demand,
And the will of the soul that unfolds.

What I was then can no longer be.
Now I grow older still.
My dreams were once a part of me
That I could not fulfill.

As I look back upon the years
That slowly slipped away.
I wasted time combating fears,
And keeping wolves at bay.

But that is now all in the past.
No need for me to worry.
My eternal flame will forever last.
I no longer need to hurry.

For I am in a place of peace,
And my soul will go on living.
I'll rest in that eternal lease
That God has promised giving.

Made in the USA
San Bernardino, CA
16 February 2020